Turn Your Screenplay into a Novel and Make Hollywood Come to You

The Authoritative Guide for Converting Your Script into a Novel

Updated 2023 with new ChatGPT Prompts!

by

RICHARD GARRISON

Hey You!

Screenwriter!

Are you frustrated with trying to accomplish the Herculean task of getting your script through the Hollywood maze?

Do you have something truly worth saying yet your message is being drowned out by the thousands (no, millions) of hopefuls, trying to accomplish the same task?

Then open your script to page one, pull up your favorite word processor, and take this incredible journey with me. In the end, you'll have a completed novel that you can sell and market and do it a hell of a lot more effectively than with a script, and in the process, you will have developed your skills as a well-rounded writer.

And, you may just have a bestseller on your hands!

~The Author

Contents

Introduction 6

The Main Premise Behind this Book......................11

What this Guide Is 14

What this Guide Isn't 16

The Process 18

    Before We Begin 20

    Convert Verbs to Past-Tense.............................22

    Embellish the Descriptions..................................36

    Determine the Scene's POV (point-of-view) Character 39

    Write From Inside the Character's Head.........53

    Master Interior Dialogue.....................................56

Finally, End Your Scenes with A Twist 58

Summarizing the Process 62

Examples of the Process at Work..........................63

Let's Talk About Dialogue.....................................86

A Word About Word Count.................................88

Layer in Backstory for Length 90

My Process...92

The Last of Us Novelization..................................95

Using ChatGPT 103

Final Thoughts..114

Notes 116

Introduction

Did you know *Die Hard*, one of the most successful franchises in movie history, was made from a novel? It's a relatively thin book entitled "Nothing Lasts Forever" and the author, Roderick Thorpe, wrote it back in 1979. You should look it up on Amazon and see if you can pick up a copy. I've always found it fascinating to read the original source material of a favorite movie. Just the other day I learned that one of my all-time favorites, *Flight of the Phoenix*, was based on a novel. I picked up a copy at the local library and gave it a read. This practice can be a very helpful learning tool for anyone considering the task of adopting his or her original screenplay into a novel.

And you probably know that *Rambo, First Blood* was based on the book by David Morrell. You should definitely read *that* if you get a chance! But be prepared for a few surprises! Morrell's main character in the book is not nearly as reluctant to kill as the character Sylvester Stallone portrays in the movie!

The point I am preparing to make is: Hollywood is terrified to risk anything new. I'm sure you know this; they don't like to gamble, certainly on an unknown. The people in charge would much rather gamble on a proven entity, something someone else has *already* gambled on. If you can create something intriguing, interesting… something that generates buzz and that anyone with an Internet connection can find on Amazon, you may just have Hollywood knocking at *your* door. Imagine that! But even if that never happens, at the very least you will have become a novelist - a REAL WRITER - and I can tell you from firsthand experience, that is a great feeling.

DIE HARD

THIS ACTION-PACKED HIT WAS ADAPTED FROM RODERICK THORP'S *NOTHING LASTS FOREVER* IN 1979, AND WAS A SEQUEL TO HIS EARLIER NOVEL, *THE DETECTIVE*. THE NOVEL, ODDLY ENOUGH, WAS NOT A HUGE SUCCESS, BUT IT DID PAVE THE WAY FOR ONE OF THE MOST SUCCESSFUL MOVIE FRANCHISES EVER.

If you're an unproduced screenwriter, regardless of how great you think your script is, you're basically standing in line with a million other poor souls who think their script is just as great. They're like an angry mob with curled scripts in their upraised hands, screaming out, "Notice me! Notice me!" But the sad reality is Hollywood doesn't notice them because there are just too many of them.

There are two BIG reasons you should seriously consider adopting your work into a novel.

First, by turning your script into a novel, you put yourself back in control of your own destiny. Once your novel hits the electronic shelves, it's available for anyone to see. It could achieve a following, and then it's off to the races!

Second, and perhaps more important, a very significant transformation occurs when you write a novel... you look at yourself differently. You become a *Novelist*. How many unproduced screenwriters can say that? I am a novelist. I am a writer. I wrote a book. All these statements will be true. People will want you to autograph a copy for them (you'll have paperbacks available on Amazon at no cost to you; this is one of the best-kept secrets on the Internet! Check out CreateSpace.com). Friends and family members will look at you differently.

And you need that. As a human being, you need the affirmation that says **I AM A WRITER** and the evidence to back it up. Your subconscious needs it. Things change after you become a published writer. Priorities become clearer. Whereas one day, you were pursuing a hobby, once you get your book on Amazon, you're no longer a hobbyist. You're an author, with an Author's Profile page. Real ISBN numbers. You're a writer. And who knows? You may just learn that you enjoy writing fiction in novel form better than you enjoy writing scripts. If that happens, embrace it. Go with it. There will always be opportunities down the road to take one of your original novels in the other direction and convert it into a screenplay. The key here is to write. That's the most important thing. Write!

Allow me to share my own story: I have written over a half-dozen scripts, had two agents in Los Angeles over the course of the years and slowly realized there had to be a better way to get my work noticed. Then one day it came to me. Instead of me knocking on Hollywood's door, trying to get their attention - just like the million or so other aspiring screenwriters - I would try something new. I would put my work in the marketplace and get Hollywood to come to me.

When you turn your screenplay into a novel, you accomplish an amazing thing...

Your original story sees the light of production, which is critical for people like us who not only yearn to create, but we yearn to entertain, to move, to inspire. We want people to experience our stories and be affected by them, entertained by them. This isn't just about selling a script, it's about moving an audience. The published novel doesn't need actors, music, lights, camera, sound. It can be enjoyed as is. It is totally self-contained.

Dr. Strangelove or: How I learned to Stop Worrying and Love the Bomb
Based on the book "Red Alert" by Peter George

George receives word that his movie is based on a book

This book is based on a single premise:

No one is going to work as hard on your behalf as you. I believe you must put yourself in control of your own destiny. That's why I turned my own scripts into books, and that's why I want to show you how to do the same.

A corollary of this premise is:

The only opinion that matters, about you and your work, is your own.

The biggest stumbling block to your own success is living in fear of what other people think. Remember William Goldman's adage: "Nobody knows anything." You can only truly trust the opinion of one person and that person is yourself.

If you have a script in the drawer, you have, right there, the basis for a novel. A novel that could quite possibly become a best-seller on Amazon. What is keeping you from turning that script, the thing you worked so hard on, into a full-length novel? The know-how? The book you're holding in your hands this very second should ease that concern. What is it, then? Fear?

Let me share a story about fear drawn from my own personal experience:

When I was in my early-twenties, I worked in the shipping department of a large factory. I was new there, and one day I got into it with one of the guys who had been around forever. Words were said, and the next thing you know, this guy, we'll call him Alfalfa – he had that strange flagpole hair thing on the top of his head – calls me outside. As in, "to fight."

I remember following him outside, my heart pounding, knees wobbling (these are POV tricks to be discussed later, btw). We step outside, he goes to throw a punch at my head, but before I can react, his fist becomes an outstretched hand, waiting for me to shake it.

"I was just kiddin'" he says to me, grinning with all the fake cheerfulness he could muster. I shook his hand, but we both knew what had just happened. He was waiting for fear to grip me and send me packing. If that had happened, if I had backed out, Alfalfa would've had my number, for as long as I worked there.

As it turned out, I had his.

The moral of this story is this: Don't let fear grip you or send you packing. Go through that door to the other side. Find out what you're capable of. You may just surprise yourself.

BAD DAY AT BLACK ROCK

HOWARD BRESLIN WROTE THE SHORT STORY *BAD TIME AT HONDA* WHICH MADE ITS WAY INTO MAGAZINE PRINT IN 1947. THAT STORY BECAME THE BASIS FOR THE 1955 FILM. THIS SUSPENSE THRILLER STARRING SPENCER TRACY BLENDED TOGETHER SUCCESSFULLY SEVERAL GENRES: CRIME, DRAMA, FILM-NOIR, AND WESTERN, AND IS CONSIDERED TODAY A TIMELESS CLASSIC.

What this Guide Is

Quite simply, this is a hands-on manual for turning your completed script into a full-length novel.

You start with nothing more than a script, preferably one you feel passionate about, and using this book to guide you, *convert* it into a novel. **How** you do that is what this book is all about.

I believe in this statement from Tom Hopkin's book, The "Official Guide to Success"

> **No one can teach you that which they have not done themselves.**

I want you to put your confidence in my ability to get you from script to finished novel. It's not difficult to do; it just requires working through your script page by page, and then going through your manuscript until you get it just the way you want it.

When we're done, you'll have a completed manuscript that you can sell via Amazon, or Lulu, or any of the other book marketplaces. You can even have on-demand hard-copies of your book printed. Take those copies to your local used bookstore and have a book-signing. Take photos, post on Facebook. You've taken the first step toward success as a real, honest-to-goodness author.

MILLION DOLLAR BABY

CLINT EASTWOOD MADE HOLLYWOOD HISTORY WHEN, AT AGE 74, HE BECAME THE OLDEST AUTEUR TO WIN AN OSCAR FOR BEST DIRECTOR. WHAT MOST PEOPLE DON'T KNOW IS THAT THE FILM IS BASED ON A COMPILATION OF SHORT STORIES BY BOXING TRAINER JERRY BOARD: ROPE BURNS, STORIES FROM THE CORNER. IT WAS PUBLISHED IN 2000.

What this Guide Isn't

This isn't a how-to guide for writing a screenplay. Something tells me you have enough of those. If you're like me, your bookshelf is probably crammed with them. And if you've reached the point where you're ready to take your writing to the next level, chances are you've learned everything you can from those.

This also isn't a how-to guide for writing a novel from scratch. Again, the bookstore's shelves are full of those as well. We'll talk about the mechanics of fiction-writing as it pertains to converting your existing script into a book narrative, and these we'll go into in detail.

Finally, this isn't a book to tell you what to do with your novel once you've written it. Those books on how to market yourself and your novel are in vast abundance on Amazon. Remember, this book has a very specific goal: to get you to a completed novel by converting your existing screenplay.

This guide may not help you write your next screenplay, but I can promise you, if you travel this journey with me and allow me to help get your script into completed novel form, you'll almost certainly be a better writer, and that better writing will be reflected in whatever you choose to write next, book or script.

REMEMBER, A STORY IS NOT ABOUT EVENTS. IT'S ABOUT A SPECIFIC CHARACTER'S **REACTIONS** TO THOSE EVENTS.

True Grit
Based on the book by Charles Portis

"Hold it right there, pilgrim. Call me fictional again and you'll think a thousand of brick fell on your head!" ~ Rooster Cogburn

The Process

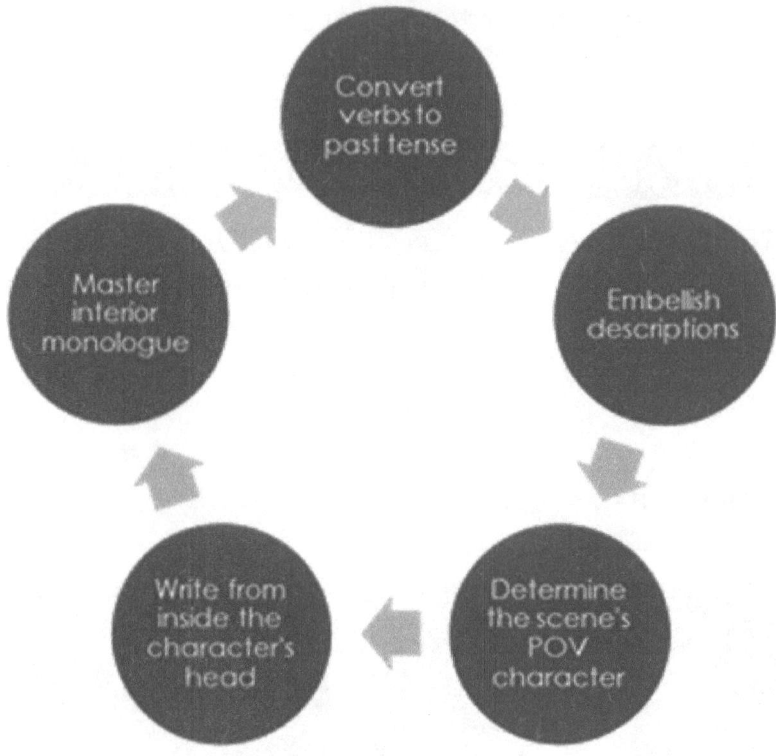

There are several primary tasks you will need to perform to convert your screenplay into a novel and we will cover each of these in detail:

1. Convert the tense from present to past
2. Embellish the descriptions
3. Determine the scene's POV (point-of-view) character

4. Write from inside the character's head
5. Master interior monologue

We're going to approach this process like a housepainter applying coats of paint to a wall.

Once we get the verbs converted, we'll keep going over the draft, adding descriptive text here and there, inserting a bit of interior monologue, throwing in a flashback if needed, etc. We'll discuss all of these finer points later in the guide.

Forrest Gump

Based on the book by Winston Groom

"Momma always said life was about turning your screenplay into a novel." ~ Forrest Gump

The first step in the process will be to convert your screenplay's present tense verbs into past tense verbs, but my experience in reading a lot of unproduced scripts has shown me a common problem many amateur scriptwriters have.

To put it bluntly, they employ way too many vague "TO BE" verbs:

```
INT. GARAGE - DAY

A skinny OLD WOMAN is working in the
attached garage of her modest home. There
is a small radio sitting on a shelf near
her. It is playing popular music.

She is in her late seventies. She's wearing
a pair of dungarees and a faded work shirt
with the sleeves rolled up. There's a pair
of red sneakers on her feet. Her hair is
short and gray and her eyes are blue.
```

This example reflects a writing style that doesn't accurately reflect the reality of what we see on screen and it just feels awkward to read. I think Robert McKee said it best in his bestselling how-to book *Story:*

Eliminate "is" and "are" throughout. Onscreen nothing is in a state of being; story life is an unending flux of change, of becoming. Not: "There is a big house on a hill above a small town." "There is," "They are," "It is," "He/She is" are the weakest possible ways into any English sentence. And what's a "big house"? Chateau? Hacienda? A "hill"? Ridge? Bluff? A "small town"? Crossroads? Hamlet? Perhaps: "A mansion guards the headlands above the village." With a Hemingwayesque shunning of Latinate and abstrate terms, of adjectives and adverbs, in favor of the most specific, active verbs and concrete nouns possible, even establishing shots come alive. Fine film description requires an imagination and a vocabulary.

So, taking McKee's advice, we might want to replace these weak "to be" verbs with stronger, specific verbs.

```
INT. GARAGE - DAY

A skinny OLD WOMAN arranges planters in the
attached garage of her modest home. A small
radio sits on a shelf nearby; the pop song
MACARENA fills the air.

She wears a pair of dungarees and a faded
work shirt. Her tiny feet sport a pair of
well-worn red keds, with one foot tapping
away to the beat of the music... (Okay, you
get the idea...)
```

You may want to take a critical look at your own work before we begin, but if you don't feel like going through your entire script fixing every weak verb instance, don't worry. You can strengthen those verbs on the fly as you change the tense from present to past, and I would strongly encourage you to do so.

Screenplays are written in present tense because they're meant to be experienced in real-time, the way a person seated in a theater experiences a movie. But most novels are written in past tense. There are a few exceptions, like the novel *Jack Wakes Up* by Seth Harwood. But because these types of novels are rare, they're a little harder to pull off. I recommend sticking to convention and writing your novel in the past tense.

Plus, there's a reason the past tense resonates with us. It seems more authentic. It's like, an amazing story has occurred, and someone feels compelled to tell it. Like the group of coworkers hanging out by the water-cooler on Monday morning. The storyteller of the group says, "I gotta tell you about this crazy thing that happened to me over the weekend," and we all pause to hear what happened.

You're going to need to go through your script page by page and convert those pesky present-tense verbs to past-tense verbs.

I recommend going through your entire screenplay and doing this first step before proceeding to the next. The good thing about doing this step first is that you'll end up with your first draft in novel format fairly quickly, although it may look skimpy in terms of word count, but we'll get to that later.

So where, for example, in this sample western horror script I have present-tense verbs, I need to convert them to past-tense verbs. I've highlighted the verbs in bold:

```
INT. SALOON - DAY
```

People **clear** themselves of the shooting lanes as they **force** their backs against the walls. Chucho's men quietly **draw** their weapons, pulling back hammers, etc.

There **is** a moment of intense silence as eyes **narrow** and teeth **set**. The stable boy **is** on pins and needles from his hiding spot beneath the stairs. No one **moves** a muscle...

And then it happens.

Chucho **goes** for his guns and Reno **hits** his elbows against his sides and two pistols **fly** into his waiting hands and in a flash he **guns** down Chucho along with one of his men standing by the door.

Just as Reno **fires**, he **rolls** over the bar, narrowly avoiding the buckshot coming from the shotgun from the man on his right. Two more of Chucho's men **go** down amid exploding wood and glass.

Reno **takes** out two more gun-wielding
targets at the top of the stairs, but his
handguns **are** clicking now, out of ammo.

Through the back door two more of Chucho's
men **burst** in, guns ablazing.
Reno **leaps** behind a capsized table and
methodically **hits** a release on the straps
connected to the middle of his chest.

Suddenly the silver cannister on his
back **pops** open and a shotgun **springs** over
his shoulder and into his hands. Before the
men can react, Reno **blasts** them into the
wall.

The place **is** filled with gunsmoke amid the
groans of dying men and the muffled cries
of huddled villagers. Reno **rises** to his
feet and **surveys** the damage.

Behind him, Chucho **crawls** through the smoke
and blood and corpses and **grabs** a gun. He
quickly **rolls** around to shoot Reno in the
back.

The stable boy **sees** this and **shouts**.

> STABLE BOY
> Senor!

First pass:

In the saloon, people **cleared** themselves of the
shooting lanes as they **forced** their backs against the walls.
Chucho's men quietly **drew** their weapons, pulling back
the hammers...

There was a moment of intense silence as eyes
narrowed and jaws **tightened**. The stable boy **was** on pins

and needles from his hiding spot beneath the stairs. No one **moved** a muscle.

And then it **happened**.

Chucho **went** for his guns and Reno **hit** his elbows against his sides and two pistols **flew** into his waiting hands and in a flash, he **gunned** down Chucho along with one of his men standing by the door.

Just as Reno **fired**, he **rolled** over the bar, narrowly avoiding the buckshot coming from the shotgun from the man on his right. Two more of Chucho's men **went** down amid exploding wood and glass.

Reno **took** out two more gun-wielding targets at the top of the stairs, but his handguns **were** clicking now. Out of ammo.

Through the back door two more of Chucho's men **burst** in, guns blazing. Reno **leapt** behind a capsized table and methodically **hit** a release on the straps connected to the middle of his chest.

Suddenly the silver canister on his back **popped** open and a shotgun **sprung** over his shoulder and into his hands. Before the men **could** react, Reno **blasted** them into the wall.

The place **filled** with gunsmoke amid the groans of dying men and the muffled cries of huddled villagers. Reno **rose** to his feet and **surveyed** the damage.

Behind him, Chucho **crawled** through the smoke and blood and corpses and **grabbed** a gun. He quickly **rolled** around to shoot Reno in the back.

The stable boy **saw** this and shouted, "Senior!"

A word of caution...

At this point, don't get hung up in the mechanics of the text, or point-of-view concerns, etc. The goal here is to just do a clean swipe of your script and get the entire story down in past tense. Sometimes, the verb form might throw you off.

 For example, I had to double-check the past tense form of the verb burst which just happens to be the same as the present tense. And, sometimes you may find a better way of expressing the action, and change, for example "teeth set" to "jaws tightened." That's okay and highly encouraged. Give yourself freedom to "explore the space," as theatrical types like to say.

SLUMDOG MILLIONAIRE

BASED ON THE NOVEL Q & A BY VIKAS SWARUP, IT BECAME THE INSPIRATION FOR THE HUGELY POPULAR AND WIDELY ACCLAIMED MOVIE: A MUMBAI TEEN FROM THE SLUMS ENDS UP WINNING A POPULAR GAME SHOW AND HAS A REALLY NIFTY DANCE SCENE WITH A BEAUTIFUL GIRL DURING THE CLOSING CREDITS. [OOPS! SPOILER ALERT!]

Still need help with converting verb tense?

Here's another example, taken from my most recent novel, THRILLER:

FADE IN:

EXT. TRINISYS TOWER - NIGHT

Fifty-stories of mirrored windows and cold steel. A granite plaque planted in the landscape like a tombstone **carries** the building's name: TRINISYS.

INT. STAIRWELL

Several uniformed guards **await** instructions. The leader, TY FALERO, an attractive, athletically-built female, **gives** the orders.

                    FALERO
          Half of you go that way.
          The others come with me.

Unbeknownst to the guards, hiding directly above them, **hangs** a FRIGHTENED MAN, late forties. His limbs **tremble** under the strain of holding himself in place.

Clenched in his teeth **is** a disk case.

The guards **split** up.

After a moment the man **drops** to his feet. He **slides** the case inside his windbreaker.

He **looks** around and then **heads** up the stairs, passing the word ROOF stenciled on the wall next to a bright red arrow.

EXT. ROOF

As the door to the roof **opens,** a searchlight from a helicopter hovering just above **sweeps** over the area. The man **lets** out a frightened gasp and **pulls** the door closed, but then **keeps** it cracked just a bit in order to see.

After a moment, the helicopter light **moves** away from him. The man, sensing his opportunity, **makes** a panicked, mad dash across the roof to the tower's shadowy edge, crouching as he **runs** in order to avoid the sweeping spotlight.

Having reached the corner of the roof, and being partially hidden in the shadows, he **pauses** to catch his breath. He then **searches** around in the darkness and after a moment he **finds** what he's looking for: a small, black PARACHUTE PACK.

Panting, he quickly **puts** it on, pausing only to give a quick look over his shoulder to where the helicopter's spotlight **roams** over another part of the building.

Being away from the searchlight, the man **stands, releases** a deep breath, and **climbs** over the guard rail. He **pauses** momentarily

to look at the ground a thousand feet below
him.

He **closes** his eyes, **bends** at the knees and
prepares to jump...

Suddenly, a voice behind him **causes** him to
freeze.

> VOICE (O.S.)
> Going somewhere?

The surprise almost **sends** him over, but he
manages to balance himself. He **turns** slowly
around...

Before him **stands** a figure, his face hidden
by the shadows.

The figure **approaches** and the first thing
seen **is** the semiautomatic pistol in his
gloved hand.

> FRIGHTENED MAN
> If you use that, they'll
> know it was murder.

The dark figure **takes** another step forward
and for the first time we **see** his face,
sharp-edged and pockmarked. His name:

CASTILLANOS.

Castillanos **stops, looks** down at the gun in
his hand.

                         CASTILLANOS
                    You know something? You're
                    right.

And he **slides** the gun into the pocket of
his overcoat.

A faint look of relief **comes** over the man's
face. He **salutes** Castillanos.

                       FRIGHTENED MAN
                    Goodbye, Detective.

And Castillanos' hand **re-emerges**, not
gripping the weapon, but in fact gripping
something else. It **catches** the frightened
man's eyes.

                         CASTILLANOS
                    Goodbye, Mr. Miller

And what **is** in Castillanos' hand **is** none
other than the parachute's rip cord.

Now here is the first-pass, novelized with the past-tense verbs:

The office tower rose in the night sky.

Fifty-stories of mirrored windows and cold steel. A granite plaque planted in the landscape like a tombstone **carried** the building's name: TRINISYS.

Several uniformed guards **awaited** instructions. The leader, Ty Falero, an attractive, athletically-built female, **gave** the orders.

"Half of you go that way. The others come with me."

Unbeknownst to the guards, hiding directly above them, **hung** a frightened man, late forties. His limbs **trembled** under the strain of holding himself in place.

Clenched in his teeth **was** a disk case.

The guards **split** up.

After a moment the man **dropped** to his feet. He **slid** the case inside his windbreaker.

He **looked** around and then **headed** up the stairs, passing the word ROOF stenciled on the wall next to a bright red arrow.

As the door to the roof **opened**, a searchlight from a helicopter hovering just above **swept** over the area. The man **let** out a frightened gasp and **pulled** the door closed, but then **kept** it cracked just a bit in order to see.

After a moment, the helicopter light **moved** away from him. The man, sensing his opportunity, **made** a panicked, mad dash across the roof to the tower's shadowy edge, crouching as he **ran** in order to avoid the sweeping spotlight.

Having reached the corner of the roof, and being partially hidden in the shadows, he **paused** to catch his breath. He then **searched** around in the darkness and after a moment he **found** what he was looking for: a small, black parachute pack.

Panting, he quickly **put** it on, pausing only to give a quick look over his shoulder to where the helicopter's spotlight **roamed** over another part of the building.

Being away from the searchlight, the man **stood**, **released** a deep breath, and **climbed** over the guard rail. He **paused** momentarily to look at the ground a thousand feet below him.

He **closed** his eyes, **bent** at the knees and **prepared** to jump...

Suddenly, a voice behind him **caused** him to freeze.

"Going somewhere?"

The surprise almost **sent** him over, but he **managed** to balance himself. He **turned** slowly around...

Before him **stood** a figure, his face hidden by the shadows.

The figure **approached,** and the first thing seen the man **saw was** the semiautomatic pistol in his gloved hand.

"If you use that, they'll know it was murder."

The dark figure **took** another step forward and for the first time the man **saw** his face: sharp-edged and pockmarked. His name: Castillanos.

Castillanos **stopped, looked** down at the gun in his hand.

"You know something? You're right."

And he **slid** the gun into the pocket of his overcoat.

A faint look of relief **came** over the man's face. He **saluted** Castillanos.

"Goodbye, Detective."

And Castillanos' hand **re-emerged,** not gripping the weapon, but in fact gripping something else. It **caught** the frightened man's eyes.

"Goodbye, Mr. Miller."

And what was in Castillanos' hand **was** none other than the parachute's rip cord.

HOW LONG SHOULD PARAGRAPHS BE?

A paragraph should represent a cohesive unit of action, description, or dialogue. What constitutes a cohesive unit is, of course, up to you. Now, having said that, the better answer is, **varied, with**

a tendency to be shorter rather than longer. The length of your paragraph constitutes the **rhythm** of the narration, just like a song. So, vary your rhythm to keep the reader from falling asleep.

SIDE NOTE:

It may be obvious, but you don't convert the verb tense in your dialogue.

So, by way of example, if you have a character named, let's say, LUKE, and you give him the following line of dialogue:

```
          LUKE
     (OVER COMLINK)
     Will you shut up and listen to
     me? Shut down all the garbage
     mashers on the detention level,
     will you? Do you copy?
```

Then this is how it appears in your novel draft:

Luke **screamed** into his comlink: "Will you shut up and listen to me!? Shut down all the garbage mashers on the detention, level, will you? Do you copy?"

Or, let's say you have a character named TRAVIS addressing an imaginary adversary in the full-length mirror of his shabby New York City apartment:

<pre>
          TRAVIS
     (to his reflection)
     You talkin' to me? You
     talkin' to me? You talkin'
     to me? Then who the hell
     else are you talking... you
     talking to me? Well I'm the
     only one here. Who the hell
     do you think you're talking
     to? Oh yeah? OK.
</pre>

And in the draft:

Travis **stood** before the mirror, with holster straps crisscrossing his bare chest, **armed** to the teeth, twirling a snub-nosed revolver around his finger like a gunslinger straight out of the old west. He **shrugged** on his army jacket and then **quick-drew** a pistol at his reflection in the mirror.

"You talkin' to me? You talkin' to me? You talkin' to me? Then who the hell else are you talking... you talking to me? Well I'm the only one here. Who the hell do you think you're talking to? Oh yeah? OK."

Total Recall

Based on the short story by Philip K.

"What do you mean based on a short story?! Keep your head down! Get to the chopper, ARGHHHH." ~ Douglas Quaid

Embellish the Descriptions

If you're used to writing screenplays, you've trained yourself to keep your descriptions sparse, only showing the most relevant details to get the point across. But in a novel, you'll want to bring life to your characters and their surroundings. For descriptions, make them breathe.

Sensory detail is the key.

How much sensory detail you put into your descriptions is entirely up to you and remember, you'll get better at this with practice.

My advice is to go overboard in the rough draft and then trim as needed in subsequent revisions.

Remember also that in a screenplay, the SLUGLINE itself is used to convey setting and time. So when it comes to writing descriptions, START WITH THE SLUGLINE!

Example:

```
FADE IN:

EXT. TRINISYS TOWER - NIGHT

Fifty-stories of mirrored windows and cold
steel. A granite plaque planted in the
landscape like a tombstone carries the
building's name: TRINISYS.
```

Embellished version:

THE CORPORATE TOWER jutted through the evening gloom like a bayonet. A ring of floodlights circling its base illuminated the tower against the brilliant night sky.

Although the tower's architectural style reflected the latest in minimalist design, the height of the scraper was anything but minimal. It loomed a thousand feet skyward and boasted sixty-seven floors concealed behind mirrored-glass walls. Even the vast campus over which the tower dominated belied its size. It, too, mocked the minimalist façade: ten lush acres of well-manicured grounds and sleek parking decks.

A small outcropping of buildings dotted the perimeter, their function serving a utilitarian nature. All of this was surrounded by what the tempered brass euphemistically referred to as a "high-energy deterrent fence."

A granite plaque implanted in the landscape like a sarcophagus carried the building's name: TRINISYS.

Another example:

```
EXT. TRINISYS BUILDING - DAY

A black limousine has just been cleared
through the main gate.
```

Embellished version:

THE NOON-DAY SKY was a serene, mystic arc of blue, with a white pearl glowing overhead, burning away the few traces of clouds left in the sky. It was unusually hot for this time of year, outside the main entrance leading into the TriniSys campus, as the stretch black limousine rolled to a stop at the security gate.

See how easy that is? Are you beginning to get the gist? In order to achieve the necessary word count, which we'll address later, we've got to allow our artistic brush to flourish. The more you do this, the easy it becomes.

PRACTICE! PRACTICE! PRACTICE!

SCARFACE

ONE OF THE MOST FAMOUS MOVIE ADAPTATIONS OF ALL TIME, SCARFACE WAS BASED ON THE BOOK OF THE SAME NAME, WRITTEN BY ARMITAGE TRAIL BACK IN 1929. THE 1983 FILM, STARRING AL PACINO, IS TYPICALLY REGARDED AS ONE OF THE BEST FILMS IN ITS GENRE. INTERESTINGLY, THE BOOK WAS A THINLY-DISGUISED BIO BASED ON THE LIFE OF AMERICAN GANGSTER AL CAPONE.

Determine the Scene's POV (point-of-view) Character

This next concept may sound blasphemous, but I believe it's absolutely critical for you to understand and adopt:

EVERY SCENE MUST HAVE A SINGULAR POV CHARACTER.

There. I said it. I'm sure there are many who would disagree, but for the purposes of easily converting your script to novel, having a singular POV character will just make your life easier, trust me.

A single POV character means we (the audience/reader) see and experience the story through THAT character's eyes, for the duration of THAT particular scene. In other words, we feel what he/she feels. We see what he/she sees. And most important, we are privy to the character's thoughts and emotions (more of this in a moment).

If you don't pick a POV character, your writing will seem at arm's length from the reader. Remember, the reader wants to experience the pain and suffering, joy and heartbreak of the main character.

It is your job as novelist to determine, given the current scene you are writing, who the POV character is. IT CANNOT BE MORE THAN ONE CHARACTER. It's okay if it switches from one character to another in subsequent scenes, but it must be consistent throughout a singular, given scene.

If your story can be told entirely from the view point of a single character, all the better. An example would be Michael Douglas's character in THE GAME. Everything we see is from his point-of-view. We never leave him. It's what helps make that movie so effective. If you can pull this off, I recommend writing your entire novel in **first-person** ("I" form), as in, "I stepped out of the shower and froze... there was a dead woman lying on my bed, painted entirely in gold..."

Most of the time, however, this is not possible to do, as the story will break from the main character and there will be scenes where that character is not present. That's why you will most likely use the **third-person** POV ("He/She"). More about this in a bit.

(If first-person is "I" and third-person is "He/She", you may be wondering what **second-person** is.

Second-person is "You" as in "You wake out of a deep sleep in a panic. Something was grabbing your leg; was it real, or just a dream?" This POV is rare in books, but a good example would be "Bright Lights Big City" by Jay McInerney.)

One other important point to remember when choosing a scene's POV character:

YOUR VILLAIN ISN'T AWARE HE/SHE ISN'T THE MAIN CHARACTER. (For that matter, neither is the kid working the valet who runs out in the rain to fetch your villain's car...) What this means is, even though your main character is in a particular scene, you may choose to have another character serve as that scene's POV...

Let's walk through some examples:

```
EXT. BEACH - NIGHT

Eddie on the beach with the girl. They make
passionate love. He falls asleep with his
arms wrapped around her.
```

Eddie finally made love to the passenger in 27F that night on the beach, with the sand luxuriously warm and soft, the moon glowing overhead like a giant clock face. The sound of the waves crashed in step with the rhythmic motion of their coupling. He was in true paradise.

A tropical breeze swept over his body, swirling her golden hair across his face. He took a moment to reflect on her beauty: the aquiline nose, the intelligent forehead, the pair of arched eyebrows - knotted at the moment, as if in deep concentration - her lips, full and moist. She was breathing hard, biting her lower lip as her body quivered beneath his. She had her arms wrapped tightly around his shoulders, a long slender leg overlapping his.

She came and he followed, their fingers digging into each other's flesh, their throats emitting moans of deep pleasure. They held each other breathlessly for a long moment, their bodies tense, and then slowly, each of them relaxed.

Eddie rolled onto his back and enjoyed the warm embrace of the sand as the ocean called out to him. He looked upward, into the star-filled night, the swaying palm trees breaching the edge of his vision. A smile lingered on his lips and his eyelids grew heavy... he was dimly aware of the girl nuzzling him, the heat of her breath on his neck, her fingers interlaced with his. Soon, without awareness, the serenity of sleep engulfed him.

That was two days ago, and he hadn't seen the girl since.

Remember, allow yourself to overwrite in the beginning, then tighten up the text in subsequent revisions.

Suppose you have a phone conversation that takes place in your script, and you INTERCUT between the two parties speaking:

INT. SARAH'S CAR - NIGHT

A puzzled look comes over her face. As she
loses herself in thought, she's jolted by
the sound of her cellular phone ringing.

She opens it.

                    VOICE (O.S.)
          Sarah?

                    SARAH
          Lou?

INT. LOU'S OFFICE

Typical editor's office of a major
newspaper. Organized chaos. Behind the desk
stands LOU, a middle-aged man as big as he
is impatient.

                    LOU
          Sarah, where do you live?

INTERCUT PHONE CONVERSATION - SARAH AND LOU

                    SARAH
          Not now, Lou. I'm in the middle
          of a --

                    LOU
          (insistent)
          Where do you live, Sarah?

In a screenplay, this is acceptable; we'll get a
shot of Lou, the stereotypical newspaper boss in
his office.

But in the novel, this is NOT acceptable.

Sarah is our POV character. She's telling the story (in this particular scene). (This is a very important concept for you to grasp so bear with me while I belabor the point.)

You wouldn't write a description of Lou's office UNLESS it was coming from inside the POV character's head:

Her mind struggled to put the pieces together. The connection seemed hidden in the misty far-reaches of her brain, but she couldn't quite penetrate it. Her thoughts were suddenly jolted back to the surface by the ringing of her cellular phone.

She looked at the number and grimaced.

"Sarah?" she heard a harsh man's voice demand.

"Lou..." She knew he was calling from the office. The man never went home. When she thought of all the stereotypical newspaper editors, Lou was the one who came to mind. No wonder the man worked all the time... he had no one else to go home to. He was heavy-set, barrel-chested; a heart-attack away from fifty. If only Lou could control his temper, thought Sarah...

"Sarah. Lemme ask you a question."

"Not now, Lou. I'm on a stake-out."

"Where do you live?" he persisted.

Sarah rolled her eyes. Oh my God, she thought, not again. "Lou..."

This problem isn't just applicable to those of us converting scripts to novels. It's a major trap that snags a lot of fiction writers. For example, see if you can tell what's wrong with this passage:

> Tom wanted to prove the old man wrong. "Okay, Mr. Doubting Thomas. Follow me down and I'll show you exactly what the hell I'm talking about."
> Tom turned and headed down the stairs.
> The old man rolled his eyes and followed...

Tom is the viewpoint character and has turned *away* from the old man. Therefore, he can't *see* the old man **roll his eyes**.

"But," I hear you protest, "that's the way it's written in the script!" You can fix problems like this without violating POV.

In this example, the old man could sigh heavily, which wouldn't violate POV. Why a heavy sigh? Because it *implies* the rolling of eyes. Picky, I know, but this is an important concept to grasp if you're to get that script turned into salable fiction. Try to sigh heavily without rolling your eyes... c'mon, I dare you ☺

You can come up with lots of ways to convey the reaction of a particular character visible on screen that wouldn't be visible by the point-of-view character:

INT. CAPTAIN WINSTON'S OFFICE – DAY

Marilyn tosses her badge on his desk.

                    MARILYN
          As far as I'm concerned, my
          involvement in this case is
          over!

She storms out. Winston stands, glaring at
the door with angry indignation.

Marilyn's heart pounded in her ears as her blood reached the boiling point. "As far as I'm concerned," she said, trying to keep her voice steady, "my involvement in this case is over!"

She yanked the badge off her belt and tossed it on the desk, spinning on her heels out the door. **She could feel his angry glare piercing her back.**

To hammer this point home, here's almost the exact same wording of the original paragraph (with one minor addition) that doesn't violate POV:

Ginny chuckled to herself: Tom was desperate to prove the old man wrong. "Okay, Mr. Doubting Thomas," he said. "Follow me down and I'll show you exactly what the hell I'm talking about."

Tom turned and headed down the stairs.

The old man rolled his eyes and followed...

See how I've changed the POV character? I'm not recommending you do this in your script. I'm merely demonstrating the technique to make a point: Pick a viewpoint character and stick with him (or her) throughout the scene.

PSYCHO

THE MOST ICONIC OF HITCHCOCK'S FILMS, HITCHCOCK BOUGHT THE RIGHTS FOR THE NOVEL ANONYMOUSLY FROM AUTHOR ROBERT BLOCK IN 1959 FOR A MERE PITTANCE. THE STORY GOES THAT HE THEN BOUGHT UP AS MANY COPIES OF THE NOVEL AS HE COULD, TO KEEP THE ENDING A SECRET FROM POTENTIAL MOVIE-GOERS.

For example:

Suppose you have a scene like this that cuts
away from your main character:

```
EXT. SHAFT ENTRANCE - ABOVE - DAY

While the CRACK, CRACK, CRACK of the whip
echoes through the canyon, our mysterious
friend has penetrated the perimeter of the
hideout and found an entry at the very top.

He is revealed to be an Indian, probably
Navajo based on his clothes, and his
movements are very stealth-like. He is
known by the name LONG HAWK. He disappears
inside the mine shaft.
```

The main character isn't even aware of what's
happening in the above scene. To do this in a
novel, I use a standard scene break convention
(* * *) preceded and followed by a carriage
return:

Harlan expertly landed the tip of the splayed leather against Reno's back in a long, thick slash. Reno's shirt ripped neatly open down his back, the edges tinged in blood. Pain rocketed through him as he clenched his teeth and clutched his eyes shut. He braced himself for worse pain to come...

    * * *

While the CRACK! CRACK! CRACK! of the whip reverberated throughout the canyon, the man who had been following the gang all across the desert plains silently made his way to the top of an outcropping of golden rock and carefully peered out.

His name was Long Hawk and he bore the contemporary Navajo clothing of the day: a buckskin waist coat, loose trousers tucked into moccasin boots at the calves, the hilt of a hunting knife above a leather sheath on his hip. He wore a bandana tied tightly around his forehead, holding into place the long hair parted evenly down the middle. A cougar fang dangled from each earlobe. His eyes were keen and sharp as they carefully scanned the narrow entrance of the mineshaft outstretched below him. He saw the idle lookouts – one on each side. Having seen everything he needed to, he quietly disappeared back into the shadows of the canyon.

Clear enough, right? But how do you handle something in the scene where there is no point-of-view character? In screenplay parlance, this is called DRAMATIC IRONY. Something happens on stage that is revealed to the audience but is unrevealed to one or more of the characters.

Here's an example of dramatic irony in the RENO NEVADA RIDES TO HELL screenplay:

```
INT. SALOON - NIGHT

The saloon turns into a regular jam session
as other men with instruments join in.
Guitarists join each other and play and
soon, young men are twirling women,
laughing, not a care in the world. Drinks
flow, men slap each other's backs.

During all this, the smoke that rises from
every lit cigar, pipe, you name it, takes
on a strange, UNEARTHLY quality. The large
fireplace in the back burns in a strange
turquoise color as well. No one notices
this unusual phenomenon.

The smoke coils around the inhabitants of
the saloon, intoxicating them with a
powerful elixir, yet none seems aware of
its effect. The mood morphs into one of
extreme celebration.

We see the smoke as it drifts up, up
through the ceiling, up through the
floorboards, up to the rooms above the
saloon...
```

And here's how I handled it in the novelization:

Down in the saloon, the festival was fully underway. Guitars had materialized and there was singing and dancing. The center of the saloon had been cleared of tables to allow for the twirling and catching of dance partners. Drinks flowed as men laughed, told stories, and slapped one another on the back.

During this, but unnoticed by all, the smoke emanating from every cigar, pipe and cigarette began to take on a strange, unearthly quality. The flames in the fireplace in the back flickered with an uncharacteristic hue. Turquoise smoke filled the room, but everyone seemed too intoxicated to notice this unusual phenomenon.

The smoke seemed to have a mind of its own as it coiled around the inhabitants of the saloon, enchanting them with its powerful elixir, yet none seemed aware of its effect on them. The mood gradually morphed into one of extreme jubilation.

The smoke drifted up, up through the ceiling, up through the floorboards of the second floor, up to the guest rooms above the saloon.

If you need to change the POV character in a scene and you don't want to convey the passage of time implied by the triple asterisks (***), then my recommendation is to use a simple, single carriage return.

Here's an example:

Jack hung up the phone, released another sigh and nodded to himself. He was beginning to feel a little better now that the police were involved. He glanced around the ransacked apartment one last time, exhaled, and then walked out the door.

[invisible carriage return]

Back in the limousine, Detective Castillanos smiled with satisfaction. This idiot college professor was going to make his job easier than he'd hoped. He slid the phone back into his pocket, looked up at the gagged, bound girl across from him and smiled.

The Thing
Based on a short story by John W. Campbell

"I don't know how. 'Cause it's different than us, see? 'Cause it's from outer space. What do you want from me? Ask the author!" ~ R.J. MacReady

How do you do this?

Easy.

You **become** the character. You put yourself in that person's shoes. You close your eyes, let your fingers rest on the keyboard, and allow yourself to **feel** the way the character would, in his or her given situation.

Here's an exercise:

You find out that your newlywed wife, a devout Christian you met on a Bible retreat, was out partying with the next-door neighbor, a bearded, long-haired biker, while you were away on a business trip.

She got stoned, got his ugly face tattoo'ed on her rear end, added a tongue-piercing just for good measure, and this is what you come home to after sixteen hours of non-stop business travel...

How do you feel?

There's a pit in the bottom of your stomach. Your heart feels like it was ripped out, trampled on by a herd of cattle. Your head is swimming, your body reeling. You can feel the blood throb in your temples…

When you're converting your script to narrative fiction, stop routinely and ask yourself, "How would I feel if I were in this situation?"

Be careful to describe it from the **inside out,** not the outside in. Outside in is how you would describe the POV character witnessing the emotions in others, but not in themselves.

If the POV character is the newlywed wife, and you're writing about her husband coming home and seeing her in this embarrassing state, describe how "his face blanched with shock and disbelief," how "his eyes widened in horror," or how "his jaw worked and made little gasping noises." Describe how he cursed, threw bottles, smashed the wedding photo, etc. But do it all from the **outside in**.

Do you see this important distinction?

Q & A

Q: Suppose something happens that shifts the character's perspective and the direction of the story. There should be a feeling or sense for the audience that it should be time for the hero to get serious, fun and games are over. How would you handle this in the novel?

A: Ask yourself, how does the main character feel? It might go something like this: "As he held the dying man in his arms, an icy resolved filled his veins. He would find the man responsible, no matter how long it took, or to what ends it drove him. He looked down at his blood-stained hands. Justice was coming, he thought, as the trembling fingers balled into fists..." Always, put yourself in your POV character's shoes and write from the inside out.

Interior dialogue isn't spoken, so don't put it in quotes, like in the following bad example:

"She was right," Earl thought to himself. "I was a miserable old fool..."

Some writers prefer to put it in *italics*, like this:

She was right, Earl realized. I was a miserable old fool...

You can get away without doing either, which is my own personal preferred approach:

Earl stood, deflated, staring after her. Who was he kidding? Lisa was right. He was a miserable old fool...

Take a look at this example, with the interior monologue in **bold**:

EXT. VERONICA'S APARTMENT - NIGHT

Jack stands at the door. It opens and he sees Veronica, dressed to the nines.

                    VERONICA
          Come in.

INT. VERONICA'S APARTMENT

Jack follows her in, admiring her figure from behind.

                    JACK
          Looks like you've been
          working out.

                  VERONICA
          Uh huh. Three days a week.

Jack arches an eyebrow as she bends down to
pick up an envelope from the counter.

                  VERONICA
          Here you go.

Jack knocked on the door and waited. A moment later, the door opened and there stood Veronica, dressed sharply in her evening gown, fastening a dangling earring onto her lobe. "Come in," she said with a smile.

Jack couldn't help keeping his eyes off her shapely figure as he followed her in. **He wanted to spin her around and plant a huge kiss on her.** Awkwardly, he heard himself say, "Looks like you've been working out."

"Uh huh," she said. "Three days a week."

In Jack's mind, they were working out right now, with her straddling him on the sofa, her dress hiked above her hips, her body writhing against him.

She picked up an envelope from the kitchen counter and unceremoniously handed it to him. "Here you go."

The divorce papers.

She needed his signature. He needed her to need him like she did when they were first married, six years ago.

Finally, End Your Scenes with A Twist

Your reader wants to be surprised, to be shocked by the unexpected. Some scenes won't require a twist, their purpose may just be to move the plot along, but whenever possible, try to give the reader a jolt they weren't expecting:

Detective Brown - an older, more distinguished-looking man - stood in the interview room with his partner, a younger detective with thinning red hair. Seated at the table before them was a bald man in a dingy tank-top.

The bald man looked up at the two detectives, his palms face down on the table. "I saw the guy standing there and I didn't want to stop."

Brown referred to his notes. "You said he was wearing some kinda clown outfit?"

"Well, no. Yes -- well, sort of."

"What do you mean, 'sort of'?"

"Well it was the clown costume, from the waist up."

The two men in suits looked at each other. Brown spoke: "Well, what was he wearing from the waist down?"

There was a pause before the bald man spoke.

"Nothing."

"You mean to tell us you stopped to pick up a strange hitchhiker in the middle of nowhere -"

"- At night," interjected the younger man.

"- At night, who was naked below the waist?"

"I told her it wasn't a good idea."

The men sighed. Detective Brown gathered himself and continued.

"Then what happened?"

"Well, he got in, we drove off and a few minutes later, I saw the knife."

"He pulled out a knife."

"Uh huh."

Again, the two men looked at each other with curious expressions. "From where?" asked the younger detective, incredulous.

"I don't know. It just came outta nowhere."

"And that's when you stopped the car?"

"Uh huh. I slammed on the brakes and got the hell outta there fast I could."

"Leaving your wife inside the car."

"I figured she'd do the same thing."

"But then the car drove off," Brown stated.

"Uh huh."

"And you've not heard from her since?"

"Well, I did get this in the mail a couple days ago."

The detective took it. It was a lapel flower. While the two men looked it over, the younger detective reached over and squeezed the connected bulb. Water shot from the flower hitting Brown squarely in the eye. He glared at his younger associate, who looked away sheepishly.

Brown turned back to the bald-headed man. "What do you think this means? Is he taunting us with this?"

"Who, the clown?"

The man shook his head.

"Why do you say that?"

He pointed at the flower in the detective's hands. "That belonged to my wife. I gave her that on our wedding night."

The two men stared at each other, speechless.

As Robert McKee famously stated, the gap between expectation and result is where story is born. When expectation and reality match, there is no story.

Picture this setting:

You're standing next to the water-cooler at work next to your friend and co-worker, Jack. Jack's got broad shoulders, perfect teeth, jet black hair. He's the guy who wears tailored-shirts, only they aren't tailored until *he* puts them on.

He begins to tell you what happened to him last night: "I'm on the rowing machine, watching Wolf Blitzer, when suddenly there's a knock at the door. I open it, and there standing in the hallway is this redhead with gorgeous green eyes, a devilish grin, wearing a full-length fur coat. Before I can open my mouth, the coat opens, falls to the ground, and I find myself standing in the presence of Venus de Milo, only this one with arms..."

Before Jack can continue, much to your chagrin, the other guy next to the cooler butts in and says, "I know what you mean! Same thing happened to me the other night. Knock at the door, I go to answer it, there's this Chinese dude standing there with a paper bag full of take out. I whip out my wallet, give the guy some money… best moo goo gai pan I ever tasted… but get this… Thing is, I didn't *order* any Chinese. Weird, huh?"

The first story is what dreams are made of, the second, indigestion. Some people have a hard time grasping just what Story is.

As storytellers, we must constantly strive to find that middle ground between expectation and result. The famous scene in MISS CONGENIALITY when Sandra Bullock first emerges from the bullpen, stunningly beautiful and decked out to the nines; all the heads turn. And then she trips and stumbles and falls flat on her face. Definitely *not* what we were expecting.

Or INGLOURIOUS BASTERDS, the charming and erudite Col. Landa, complimenting the French farmer on his exquisite milk and beautiful daughters, only to direct his men moments later to fire their machine guns into the floorboards where innocent women and children are hiding.

If you don't strive to deliver the unexpected, you won't be able to engage your readers and your work will come off seeming banal and familiar. As an artist and author, you don't want that.

Summarizing the Process

Let's review the critical steps involved:

1. Convert present-tense verbs to past-tense
2. Embellish the descriptions using sensory detail
3. Choose your point of view character in the scene and stick with him or her
4. Write from inside the character's head
5. Master interior dialogue and avoid point-of-view violations

Magic

Based on the creepy novel by William Goldman

"Say hello to my little friend." ~ Corky the magician

Examples of the Process at Work

Let's take a scene from a produced script, and actually go through the process step-by-step to further illustrate how this works.

The first example is from INGLOURIOUS BASTERDS, the 2009 film by Quentin Tarantino. (Note: For the purpose of instruction, I'm not using the published script which differs from the screen version, but instead scripting the scene as it appears on film.)

The scene we'll be using is the cat-and-mouse exchange between Col. Hans Landa (played by Christoph Waltz) and Bridget von Hammersmark (Diane Kruger).

```
INT. SHOSANNA'S OFFICE - NIGHT

Shosanna's cinema manager's office. It's
small, cluttered, and dominated by a desk.

They both enter.

Col. Landa closes the door behind him.

He pulls up a chair across from the desk.

                COL. LANDA
          Have a seat, Fräulein.

She lowers herself in the chair.
```

                    COL. LANDA
              May I?

He takes her drink from her hands and
places on the shelves behind her.

Col. Landa takes the leather overcoat
hanging on the coat rack and drapes it over
the back of Bridget's chair.

                    COL. LANDA
              Mademoiselle Mimieux
              allowed me to set up camp
              in her office for the time
              being.

Instead of moving around to the other side
of the desk, opposite her, the S.S. Colonel
pulls another little chair over and places
it in front of the fräulein.

He sits, their knees almost touching. He
smiles ...

                    COL. LANDA
              Let me see your foot.

                    BRIDGET
              I beg your pardon?

Patting his lap.

                    COL. LANDA
              Put your foot in my lap.

                    BRIDGET
              Hans, you embarrass me.

He says nothing but instead motions
elaborately to his lap.

The nervous fräulein lifts up her strappy
dress shoe enclosed foot and places it in
the colonel's lap.

The Colonel very delicately unfastens the
thin straps that hold the fräulein's shoe
on her foot ...

... He removes the shoe ...

... Leaving only the fräulein's bare foot
...

THEN ...

                    COL. LANDA
            (pointing)
            Could you please reach into
            the right pocket of my
            coat...
            (enjoying every second of
            this)
            And give me what you find
            there...

Bridget reaches into the pocket of the coat
draped behind her ...

... Digs inside the pocket with her
elegantly gloved hand ...

... And finds what the Colonel has hidden
for her ...

She looks up at the Colonel ...

He nods.

Bridget pulls out the pretty dress shoe,
the one left behind at the basement tavern.

                    COL. LANDA
          May I?

He extends a hand and Bridget hands it to
Landa.

He slips it on her foot ...

... It fits like a glove.

Bridget knows she's BUSTED.

Col. Landa smiles.

                    COL. LANDA
          Voila. What's that American
          expression... "If the shoe
          fits... you must wear it."

                    BRIDGET
          What now, Colonel?

A long moment passes as the two look at
each other, and then ...

Hans LUNGES forward, putting his strong
mitts around Bridget von Hammersmark's
lily-white, delicate neck, and with all the
violence of a lion in mid-pounce, SQUEEZES
with all his might.

Bridget's face turns tomato RED, as the
VEINS in her face BULGE and her esophagus
is CRUSHED in his GRIP.

With a violent YANK, he JERKS her TO THE
FLOOR. She TUMBLES out of the chair, Landa
never releasing his GRIP around her throat.
Now fully on top of her, he BEARS DOWN,
SQUEEZING THE VERY LIFE OUT OF HER.
Everything he has, he brings to bear on the
elegant lady's neck.

She struggles, to no avail. Eventually her
limbs go limp.

Dead.

He releases the grip around her throat. His
hands are trembling.

He stands, picks up the phone and calmly
dials a number.

                    COL. LANDA
               (into the phone)
               The guy in the white
               smoking jacket.

Now, the first pass at novelization: **changing the verb tense:**

Col. Landa opened the door to the cinema manager's
office. It was a small, cluttered room dominated by a large
desk. He invited Bridget in and shut the door behind her.

He pulled up a padded high-back chair near the door.
"Have a seat, Fräulein," he said and motioned to it.

Bridget lowered herself in the chair.

"May I," he asked, taking her drink from her and setting it down somewhere behind her.

He took the leather overcoat hanging on the coat rack and draped it over the back of Bridget's chair.

"Mademoiselle Mimieux allowed me to set up camp in her office for the time being."

Instead of moving around to the other side of the desk, opposite her, the S.S. Colonel pulled another chair over and placed it in front of the fräulein.

He sat down, so close to her that their knees almost touched. He smiled pleasantly. "Let me see your foot," he Colonel said.

"I beg your pardon?"

The Colonel patted his thigh. "Put your foot in my lap."

"Hans, you embarrass me."

He said nothing but instead motioned elaborately to his lap.

The nervous fräulein lifted up her strappy dress shoe-enclosed foot and placed it in the colonel's lap.

The Colonel very delicately unfastened the thin straps that held the fräulein's shoe on her foot ...

... He removed the shoe ...

... Leaving only the fräulein's bare foot ...

And then the Colonel motioned to something behind her. "Could you please reach into the right pocket of my coat and hand me what you find there."

Bridget reached into the pocket of the coat draped behind her. She dug inside the pocket with her elegantly gloved hand, until finally landing upon what the Colonel had hidden for her.

She looked up at the Colonel.

He nodded.

Bridget pulled out the pretty dress shoe, the one left behind at the basement tavern.

"May I?" asked Hans, extending a hand.

Bridget handed the shoe to him.

He slipped it on her foot.

It snapped over her heel like a glove.

Bridget knew she was busted.

Col. Landa smiled. "Voila. What's that American expression... 'If the shoe fits... you must wear it.'"

"What now, Colonel?"

A long moment passed as the two looked at each other, and then suddenly...

Hans lunged forward, putting his strong mitts around Bridget von Hammersmark's lily-white, delicate neck, and with all the violence of a lion in mid-pounce, squeezed with all his might.

Bridget's face turned tomato red, as the veins in her face bulged and her esophagus collapsed in his grip.

With a violent yank, he jerked her to the floor. She tumbled out of the chair, Landa never releasing his grip around her throat. Fully on top of her, he bore down, squeezing the very life out of her. Everything he had, he brought to bear on the elegant lady's neck.

She struggled, but to no avail. Eventually her limbs went limp.

Dead.

He released the grip around her throat. He stood, his hands trembling.

Calmly, he picked up the phone and dialed a number.

"The guy in the white smoking jacket," he said into the phone."

Looks like a novel, doesn't it? But we still have work to do. Next pass, **embellish the descriptions** and **chose the scene's POV character**. See if you can tell which character I chose...

Col. Landa opened the door to the cinema manager's office which lay just down the hall from the main lobby. He held the door open and Bridget entered, struggling to keep her panic under control. She looked around. Overfilled shelves with books and papers lined the walls. She noted the brooding ambience: dark furniture, blood-red drapes, hardwood floors. A large desk of rich mahogany dominated one corner of the room.

She waited nervously as the S.S. Colonel shut the door behind her.

He pulled up a padded high-back chair near the door. "Have a seat, Fräulein," he said and motioned to it.

His conversational tone and pleasant demeanor were unsettling. She prayed her nervousness would not betray her as she lowered herself into the chair.

"May I," he asked, taking her drink from her and setting it down somewhere behind her.

She could hear him moving around behind her and she became aware of his draping a leather coat over the back of her chair. She wanted desperately to return to her companions in the lobby but she did her best to feign that nothing was wrong.

"Mademoiselle Mimieux allowed me to set up camp in her office for the time being," he said, almost sounding apologetic.

Instead of moving around to the other side of the desk, which she had expected, the S.S. Colonel surprised her by pulling up another chair and positioning it in front of her.

He sat down facing her, so close that his knees almost touched hers. She tried hard not to react.

He looked at her and smiled pleasantly. "Let me see your foot."

"I beg your pardon?" she heard herself say.

The Colonel patted his thigh. "Put your foot in my lap." His tone had lost a hint of its pleasantness.

"Hans," she said, forcing a blush. "You embarrass me."

He said nothing but instead motioned to his lap; elaborately. No, Bridget corrected herself; ominously.

She swallowed hard and then lifted up her strappy dress shoe-enclosed foot and placed it gently on the Colonel's lap.

The Colonel very delicately unfastened the thin straps that held the fräulein's shoe on her foot. She could feel the blood freezing in her veins.

With a sensuality reserved for lovers, he eased the shoe off her bare foot.

Bridget's heart threatened to burst from her chest.

The Colonel motioned to something behind her.

"Could you please reach into the right pocket of my coat and hand me what you find there."

Bridget couldn't help but notice the evil twinkle in the German officer's eye.

She reached into the pocket of the coat draped behind her. With trepidation biting at her resolve, she dug inside the pocket with her gloved hand, until finally landing upon what the Colonel had hidden for her.

Her shoe.

She looked up at the Colonel, her heartbeat pounding in her ears. Fear was easing its icy grip around her.

The Colonel arched an eyebrow and nodded.

She pulled the pretty dress shoe she'd left behind at the basement tavern out of the pocket.

"May I?" Hans asked, extending a hand, his voice almost cheery.

Bridget's trembling arm extended the shoe out to him.

He took it and slipped it on her foot.

It snapped over her heel with the satisfying pop of a perfect fit. A pop ordinarily pleasing to a woman's ears.

This pop meant something else entirely.

Bridget knew she was in trouble.

Col. Landa smiled. "Voila. What's that American expression... 'If the shoe fits... you must wear it.'"

She could feel her lower jaw quiver as she managed to ask: "What now, Colonel?"

A long moment passed as she watched the Colonel smile pleasantly at her. Perhaps there was hope of surviving this evening after all...

But then, suddenly, Hans lunged forward, throwing his flayed fingers around Bridget's neck. The swift, brutal action surprised her, and her hands went to his. She looked into his crazed eyes, his maddening grimace: she knew he was squeezing with all the strength he could muster.

She felt her face turn red, felt the veins in her temples bulge, could feel the horrible collapse of her esophagus in his vise-like grip.

Hans grunted, and with a violent wrench, she felt herself yanked out of the chair and jerked to the floor. She struggled against the Colonel's fingers, but they only tightened their death grip around her throat. Fully on top of her, he bore down; she could feel him squeezing the very life out of her. Saliva dripped from the corners of the man's contorted mouth; she saw his cloud-covered eyes bulge. He was squeezing with every ounce of strength he could muster.

The room grew dark as the final vapor of life's breath left her body.

Colonel Landa noticed that the fräulein's body had become limp. He released the grip around her throat and caught his breath. He panted heavily, savoring the feeling of exhilaration coursing through his body. Finally he stood, his hands trembling.

He walked over to the desk, picked up the phone and dialed a number.

"The guy in the white smoking jacket," he said calmly into the phone.

This second example is a scene from the 1997 movie, *The Game* starring Michael Douglas and

Deborah Kara Unger. To make the narrative more effective, let's convert this one into **first-person** perspective.

```
INT. CABIN - NIGHT

FIRE in the fireplace.  Christine tends a
metal pot over the flames. Nicholas sleeps
slumped in a low chair. Christine passes
with the pot. Nicholas awakens,
disoriented, searching for familiarity. He
sits forward...

Christine's in the candle-lit kitchenette.
He watches her, grim. She makes coffee. He
sits back.

                    CHRISTINE
               What?

Christine comes over and gives him a mug of
coffee.

                    CHRISTINE
               What did you say?

                    NICHOLAS
               I didn't say anything.

He gets up, walks, sipping coffee.
Christine watches him.

Nicholas stares at FAMILY PHOTOS on the
mantle.
```

                    CHRISTINE
          (sad, unsure)
          My name's not Christine.
          It's not my real...

                    NICHOLAS
          Who the fuck cares?

He doesn't even look at her, picks up a
PHOTO: FATHER and YOUNG NICHOLAS, holding
up fish. Nicholas rubs the dust off his
father's face.

                    CHRISTINE
          It's just money. You should
          be glad you're alive.

                    NICHOLAS
          It might be best if we
          didn't talk.

                    CHRISTINE
          All I mean is... someone
          like you...

                    NICHOLAS
          How many times have you
          done this? I'm interested.

                    CHRISTINE
          What?

                    NICHOLAS
          Scams, con games. How
          many?

                    CHRISTINE
          I don't know. A lot.

                    NICHOLAS
          Whatever kind of nickel-
          and-dime shit you did
          before, this is more than
          just me. Your friends
          raided pension plans, and
          payrolls... they took just
          over six-hundred million.
          You ruined people's lives.

Christine looks sick and truly scared. The
CELLULAR CHIRPS.

Nicholas goes to pick it up off a table.

                    NICHOLAS
               (into cellular)
          Yes.

                    SUTHERLAND (v.o.)
               (from cellular)
          I got your message. I was
          disturbed, to say the
          least...

Christine stands.

                    CHRISTINE
          Who is it?

                    NICHOLAS
               (into cellular)
          What do we do?

                    SUTHERLAND (v.o.)
               (from cellular)
          I've been on the phone for
          an hour already. Nicholas,
          your funds are intact.
          Nothing's been touched.

                    CHRISTINE
               (worried, insistent)
          Who is it?

                    NICHOLAS
               (still into cellular)
          What do you mean? I
          checked them myself. I made
          the calls...

                    SUTHERLAND (v.o.)
          Nothing's changed. I'm
          telling you, not a cent is
          unaccounted for...

                    NICHOLAS
               (cups phone, to Christine)
          My lawyer... says nothing's
          missing.

She shakes her head ominously.

                    CHRISTINE
               (a fearful whisper)
          He's in on it...

Nicholas stares at Christine, trying to
comprehend...

                    SUTHERLAND (v.o.)
          I don't know what's
          happening, but stay where
          you are till I get to you.
          Give me your precise
          location...

                    CHRISTINE
          Sutherland's in on it.

                    SUTHERLAND (v.o.)
          I'll come there. Hold on,
          Nicholas, I have another
          call. Tell me where you
          are.

Nicholas lowers the phone, pushes
DISCONNECT, afraid.

                    NICHOLAS
          We have to get out of here.

The PHONE CHIRPS again. Nicholas looks at
it, flicks a switch on the side, silencing
it. He sits, sickened.

                    NICHOLAS
          How did they get to him?
          Why didn't you tell me?

She lights a cigarette, backing toward the
kitchenette.

                    CHRISTINE
          Mm... I wouldn't worry
          about it.

                    NICHOLAS
          What... what do you mean?

                    CHRISTINE
          It's out of your hands.

He looks up, trying to figure. His head
lulls...

He takes a breath, looks at his trembling
hands. Drugged.

He looks around, confused... spots the
COFFEE CUP, realizes.

With a CRY of RAGE, he LUNGES toward
Christine, but comes up short, toppling a
shelf, contents CRASHING DOWN...

Nicholas rolls, pained, clutching his
throat, taking air in RASPING GULPS. He
crawls, swings his fist, slams a table...

                    CHRISTINE
          Cellular calls can be
          intercepted, you know.

Christine backs to avoid, hefts a heavy
cooking POT in case.

She maneuvers, steps over him. He grabs,
blindly...

She scoops up the dropped PHONE and crosses
away.

                    CHRISTINE
              (cigarette 'tween lips)
          All those calls you made,
          to B of A, France,
          Switzerland... you were
          talking to my people.
              (hits REDIAL on cellular)
          You filled the blanks.
          Access codes, passwords,
          stuff even your lawyer
          didn't have -- but we have
          it now.

Nicholas tries to stand, falls, clutching
his gut, CRYING OUT in great pain, frothing
at the mouth.

                    CHRISTINE
          It's over, Nicholas.
          Goodbye.

THE ROOM SPINS round and round, spinning
OUT OF CONTROL.

FADE TO BLACK

BREATHING... then a STRUGGLE... POUNDING,
KICKING...

Here's the first pass at novelization:

There was a fire burning in the fireplace. Christine
tended a metal pot over the flames. I was slumped in a low
chair; I guess I had fallen asleep.

She passed by with the pot as I looked around the cabin, trying to remember where I was, searching for something familiar.

I sat forward. The woman was in the candle-lit kitchenette, making coffee. Groggily I sat back...

"What?" she called out.

She strode toward me and handed me a mug.

"What did you say?" she asked.

"I didn't say anything."

I took the mug and lifted it to my lips. The hot liquid provided little comfort as the reality of what had happened that night came back to haunt me.

I stood, feeling anxious. I should be doing something. I stopped and stared at the familiar photos lining the mantle.

"My name's not Christine," she said, her voice low, contrite. "It's not my real name..."

"Who the fuck cares?" I heard myself mutter. I was staring at a black and white photo, me and Father, fishing. I used my thumb to clear the dust from my old man's face. If he could see me now...

I shook my head in disgust.

"It's just money," she rambled on. "You should be glad you're alive."

Glad I was alive? Did this *two-bit tramp* know how close I was to strangling the life blood out of her?

"It would be best if we didn't talk," I managed to say calmly.

"All I mean is," she continued, "someone like you..."

I put the photo back on the mantel. Without turning, I stiffened. "How many times have you done this?" I asked. "I'm interested."

"What?" she asked, her voice sounding defensive.

"Scams. Con games. How many?"

I watched her from the corner of my eyes as her gaze fell to the wooden floor.

"I don't know. A lot."

I turned to face her, so that she couldn't fail to miss the look of pure disgust in my eyes. "Whatever kind of nickel-and-dime shit you did before, this is more than just me. Your friends raided pension plans, payrolls... They took just over six-hundred million."

As her eyes widened with – what? Excitement? Surprise? I couldn't tell which – I said, my anger boiling: "You ruined people's lives."

Her face paled and she turned away. Was she acting or did she truly feel remorse? As I struggled to discern which, the cellphone on the table chirped. I rushed to pick it up.

"Yes?" I asked, praying for a miracle to wake me from this nightmare.

It was Sutherland. Thank God! His voice sounded reserved, cautious: "I got your message. I was disturbed, to say the least."

Christine made a vague movement in an effort to catch my eye. Her voice was insistent. "Who is it?" she whispered.

I ignored her. "What do we do?" I asked Sutherland.

"I've been on the phone for an hour already." He sucked in a breath, "Nicholas, your funds are intact. Nothing's been touched."

What? *Nothing's been touched?* It didn't make any sense...

Christine made another attempt to grab my attention. "Who is it?" she asked again, her voice deep with worry.

I turned away. "What do you mean?" I challenged my lawyer. "I checked them myself. I made the calls..."

"Nothing's changed. I'm telling you, not one red cent is unaccounted for..."

Unable to deal with Christine's look of distress, I lowered the phone, cupped the mouthpiece with my hand.

"My lawyer," I said. "He says nothing's missing."

Her face went pale. She shook her head, eyes wide with fear.

"He's in on it," she whispered.

I stared at her as the blood rushed out of my body, my jaw dropping open.

Sutherland continued to speak, "I don't know what's happening," he said, "but stay where you are till I get to you."

I put the phone back to my ear, my hand trembling.

"Give me your precise location..." he said.

I looked up; Christine was still shaking her head no. "Sutherland's in on it."

Sutherland's voice continued: "I'll come there. Hold on, Nicholas, I have another call. Tell me where you are."

I gave one last glance to Christine's frightened face and lowered the phone. Almost in a trance, I felt myself close it, disconnecting the call.

Whatever was happening, couldn't be real.

I swallowed hard.

"We have to get out of here."

The phone chirped in my hands. I looked down at it, flicked the power button off. I felt my knees give, felt myself collapse into the nearby chair, my gut twisted. A wave of nausea was curdling inside me.

"How did they get to him?" I asked myself. I looked at Christine. "Why didn't you tell me?"

Her demeanor was different. Shockingly different. In a word: apathetic. Where had that look of concern and fright disappeared to? She was now neither of those things.

She casually brought a cigarette to her lips as she backed her way toward the kitchen.

"Mm... I wouldn't worry about it."

I could feel my throat tighten. My vision was growing blurred. What was happening to me?

I heard myself mutter: "What... what do you mean?"

"It's out of your hands."

I tried to focus on her, but my head seemed to weight more than my neck could support. I took in a deep breath, looked at my hands... they were trembling.

I looked around the dizzying room, the walls skewed. My eyes landed on the coffee mug on the table.

Then it came to me.

The bitch drugged me.

Rage roiled through me and sheer bloodlust filled my veins. I wanted to strangle her, tried to, but found myself toppling down as the room spiraled out of control.

I rolled on the ground, clutching my cramping gut. I felt my intestines trying to bubble up from my stomach. I swung wildly, hitting nothing but air.

"Cellular calls can be intercepted, you know."

I grappled for her blindly, but the last ebbs of consciousness were receding fast.

"All those calls you made, to B of A, France, Switzerland... You were talking to us. My people."

No! NO! I tried to stand, had to get to a phone... so much at stake, lives, innocent lives ruined...

"It's over, Nicholas. Goodbye."

On hands and knees, the room spinning wildly, I made one last lunging attempt to grab at her, but pain and darkness overwhelmed me, and unconsciousness consumed me, and the next thing I knew I was no longer in the waking world.

Is this ageless prose? No, but that's hardly the point. Your final product will be different from mine in the end because we're both different individuals. We're unique. No two people will write it the same way because no two people look at the world the same way.

But what these examples intend to illustrate is *how* you convert script page to novel page. You start with a point-of-view character, drop into their skin, and experience the world through their eyes.

Let's Talk About Dialogue

When converting screen dialogue to novel dialogue, remember to give each new speaker their own paragraph.

Here's an example:

Mary Hatch looked out the window and suddenly her heart was filled with joy. George Baily was out front, walking back and forth by the front gate. She was about to call out to him, but his apparent indecision caused her to hesitate. He seemed to be struggling with something.

"What are you doing, picketing?" she finally called out to him, in as pleasant a voice she could deliver.

He glanced up and saw her and without smiling he said, "Hello, Mary. I just happened to be passing by."

"Yes, so I noticed." She tried to temper her enthusiasm. "Have you made up your mind?"

"How's that?"

"Have you made up your mind?" she asked.

"About what?"

"About coming in. Your mother just phoned and said you were on your way over to pay me a visit."

Dialogue is like a tennis match between two players, and each paragraph is that player's attempt to get the ball over the net.

(Note the POV in the above scene: We've all seen *It's a Wonderful Life* with Jimmy Stewart and Donna Reed, and we know that George Baily is the main character. But in this particular scene, the POV shifts from George to Mary, and we experience the scene from her point-of-view.)

Sometimes you can have the same character deliver two or more lines of dialogue in the same paragraph and there's a very important reason you would want to do this.

Example:

Jack turned to the large man, leveling the gun at his mid-section: "You're going to step off this elevator and I'm going to walk out right behind you." He jammed the gun into his ribs and added, "And if you make any sudden moves, I'll kill you."

In the same paragraph conveys **immediacy**. The action that separates the dialogue has a certain sense of urgency.

If you break the action (bit) into its own paragraph, it conveys the passage of time:

Jack turned to the large man and leveled the gun at him.

"You're going to step off this elevator and I'm going to walk out right behind you."

He stuck the muzzle into the man's ribs.

"And if you make any sudden moves," Jack added, "I'll kill you."

A Word About Word Count

When we move from screenplay to novel, our measurement for length changes.

For screenplays, we measure length in terms of **pages**. For novels, we use **word count**. The ideal length for a spec script is around 100 pages, give or take a few. The ideal word count for your novel from script is **50,000** words.

That should be the target you shoot for. Why? Most mainstream publishers will regard anything less as a *novella* and hence may treat your work differently. 50,000 words makes for a nice-sized novel and an engaging 200-plus page book.

Having said that, if you fall a few thousand words short, don't worry about it. A lean, tight novel that moves at a fast clip is beauty in itself. But if you're hovering below 40,000 words – definitely the novella range – I would recommend spending some time to see if you've cut anything too short. Descriptions, dialogue, interior monologue, etc. Don't be wordy just for the sake of length, but if your novel is too short, chances are you haven't given ample attention to some of the crucial details.

As a guide to help you get there, remember that a page of script equates roughly to one minute of screen time. This means that, for the 100-page average screenplay, the ideal would be to have each page of script translate to 500 words.

But if you focus on this goal in the beginning, you'll just become discouraged. Take my advice and don't worry about word count until you get into the later drafts of your novel.

ABOUT CHAPTER LENGTH:

A chapter in your novel from script could be a single scene, or a combination of scenes representing a unit of action.

A good rule of thumb is to keep your chapters under 2,000 words. That's about 25 chapters for a short novel. But, like paragraphs, pacing is the key.

Try to avoid long chapters, as 2,000 words is about the most a reader can digest without catching their breath. Some of your chapters may be three to five pages long; others, perhaps only a page. The days of ten 15-page chapters of a one-hundred-and fifty-page novel you used to see the golden-age of paperbacks is over. (Just my opinion.)

Layer in Backstory for Length

It may just turn out that your script is just too tight for you to reach the 50,000-word mark. If that's the case, and you feel it needs the added length to be regarded a complete novel, then I suggest layering in backstory.

Backstory consists of the incidents that occurred before your story proper begins. You can layer in backstory wherever you need, but the best place is right after a high point in tension has been reached. This will keep the reader in suspense, eagerly waiting to return to the main story to find out how that earlier tension is resolved.

Here's an example:

Suppose you have a script where the main character, Hector, is intent upon killing his brother for the sole purpose of obtaining his brother's wife, whom he lusts after...

After a peak in the action, try layering in some backstory:

Hector first met and fell in love with Rhonda at a wedding. He couldn't remember who's at the moment – wait, that's right, it was hers. She'd just tied the knot with some pompous writer she'd met in Greece while on his book-signing tour. His name was Jules and it bothered Hector how the man threw his money around, leaving behind the insinuation, though he never said it, that Hector should make an effort to someday pay him back.

He knew that only the untimely death of Rhonda's husband could grant Hector the opportunity to be with the woman of his dreams. But Jules was like an older brother to Hector, so much so, that they even shared the same mother and father.

Killing him would not be easy, but then he reminded himself, nothing worth having ever is. Except for this job - high-rise apartment manager - which Hector hated. Having to work for Jules was almost as painful as having to watch him make love to his beautiful wife, which he did every Saturday and Sunday, and most weeknights in between.

This process of putting the story on hold, right after a climatic upbeat, affords a lot of opportunity to layer in backstory, flesh out the motivations of the characters and give the novel extra length.

My Process

I start with Notepad - I don't want any artificial
editor looking over my shoulder - and I turn to
page one of my script. If the first slugline is: EXT.
STATE HIGHWAY - NIGHT, I want to know what
kind of night it is. Is it starry, clear, cold, hot, dry...
etc. I put down whatever comes to mind,
keeping in sync with what I had originally
intended:

A thousand stars littered the brilliant night sky...

...shit like that. I may write it half a dozen ways.
I'm just trying to get the truest sense of what the
film, if it were made, would show. Clouds, wind,
whatever comes to mind. And is it early evening
or late? Predawn? Is there a red tinge on the
horizon? Summer or fall? All this gets down on the
page and I'm not making any judgments about
how it reads. If a phrase comes out sounding
particularly nice, I'll put carriage returns around it;
I might want to use it later on.

Next, the highway. Is it long and straight? Lonely?
Are we in the heartland or the city?

A ribbon of desolate highway stretched out into
darkness. Rolling farmland flashed by under the translucent
moon-lit sky.

Does it sound corny, obtuse, overly-literary? I don't care at this point. I'm just trying to get the motor going, the pistons pumping.

Soon, I'll need to reveal the character in the scene, and if he or she is the scene's protagonist (which could be different scene-to-scene) I'll want to straight-away drop into the character's head, show some inner monologue, something to tell the reader THIS CHARACTER IS IMPORTANT, THIS IS OUR FOCAL POINT CHARACTER:

Ellie had her elbow resting on the open window of her truck, letting the wind rush through her hair, enjoying the sensation on the nape of her neck. She steered casually with the wrist of her other hand, her head titled and relaxed. The truth was she loved to drive, loved to take long trips alone, to allow herself time to think, to reflect. A song played on the radio and she sang along to it absent-mindedly, a cappella, her lilting voice filling the cabin of her F-150.

I'll stay in Ellie's head all through the scene, even if another character is introduced, because it's ELLIE'S SCENE. I drop into her head, ask what does she see? What does she feel? The answers will pop out as sentence fragments on the screen: She feels calm, relaxed, assured... She may be a little tired from driving and rub her eyes, or yawn, or glance quickly at the map to indicate she's never been down this way before, whatever the scene requires. She may be struck by a memory, long drives with her father as a kid, always eager to explore, to go places she's never been. All this gets transferred to the screen, no judgments or considerations of phrasing.

If a new character is introduced, what is Ellie's reaction to him/her? How does she describe him, who does he remind her of, what's her first impression?

> The old man looked surprisingly virile for his age, a lifetime spent working with his hands under a hot sun. She instantly knew she liked him, and an image of her father sprang to mind.

I'll continue on like this until I get to the end of the scene, and then I'll transfer it to the word processor, with its judgmental squiggly lines, and try molding it into some kind of shape, some kind of narrative. Something that resembles the text of an actual novel. I won't let myself get too bogged down in trying to perfect it, it's way too early for that, but I want words on a page that encourage me to go on, like dipping my toe in the pool before diving in completely.

The Last of Us Novelization

For some time, I've been engaged in the arduous task of turning a console game into a novel. Luckily for me, I chose one of the best stories – and most popular games – that's ever been produced, THE LAST OF US, by the brilliant mind of Neil Druckmann:

If you're not familiar with the game, I highly recommend you check it out. My first experience, since I didn't own a console, was watching the entire game on a YouTube channel, all ten hours' worth. Man, what a ride!

Basically, what I would do is watch the video, pause, and then write what I witnessed in novel form. I've never seen the script used for the game, but I can recreate the script in my head by watching the scenes unfold, the same as I did for INGLOURIOUS BASTERDS, and THE GAME, in a previous chapter.

I want you to watch the opening scene (found here: THE LAST OF US REMASTERED FULL MOVIE [HD] – credit to 【XCV//】 for recording) and then read my interpretation that follows:

Joel Shepard got home late. He pulled his beat-up Chevy pick-up into the driveway, turned off the engine and sat for a moment, exhausted, under a full moon in the dead of a Texas night. He grabbed the keys from the ignition and looked glumly at the dark house before him: a two-story tract home on a half-acre lot with wood-siding. A rocking chair sat on the narrow porch by the front door. He grunted, opened the truck door and climbed out. It was another red-letter day at the job site. The crew was now down to five and was six weeks behind. And the client, now at the end of his rope, was threatening lawsuits.

As he walked heavily to the front door, his cell phone rang. He glanced down, saw the number and cursed to himself. More problems. It didn't seem this day would ever end. He shook his head as he flipped it open. "For chrissake. What now?"

It was his brother Tommy.

"Just got off the phone with Lance," Tommy sighed. "Whatever's going around, apparently he's got it too."

"So," Joel said, his blood pressure rising. "No tile guy."

"No tile guy," his brother confirmed.

"That's just..." He was on the verge of swearing but didn't have the energy. Instead, he fumbled with the keys in his hand. "This whole job's going south, Tommy. And the goddamn contractor is nowhere to be found."

"If he's sick, he's sick. Not much you can do --"

Joel opened the door to his house and stepped inside. "Tommy. Tommy," he interrupted. "He is the contractor." He caught his temperature rising and lowered his voice. "He is the contractor, okay? I can't lose this job."

"What is it about 'sick' you don't understand?"

Joel caught a glimpse of the ten-year-old asleep on the sofa. "I understand."

"Look. I'll call around, find someone."

"Let's talk about this in the morning, okay?" He flipped the switch by the door. The girl stirred as a soft glow of light filled the den.

"Hell, maybe I'll do it. How far along was he?"

"We'll talk about it in the morning."

"Sure."

"All right," Joel said. "Goodnight." He flipped the phone off and tossed the keys on the coffee table.

Yawning, the young girl sat up on one elbow. "Hey," she said, squinting up at him.

"Scoot," was all he could muster. She made room for him and he let his body collapse into the leather cushions.

"Fun day at work?"

Joel took a long look at her. She was in her plaid, thread-bare pajama bottoms and had one tee-shirt over another. Leather bracelets encircled her wrist and she wore a choker with beads around her neck. Her name was Sarah and she had a style all her own. Wheat-colored hair like her mother's which she preferred to keep short, an aversion to make-up, to boys, and especially dresses.

But that wonderful Texas drawl of hers? That was all Joel.

Her father gave her a sideways glance. "What are you still doing up?" He propped his head upright with tired fingers. "It's late."

"Oh crud what time is it?" She spun around and looked at the clock on the wall above the sofa.

Joel knew what time it was without lifting a muscle. "It's way past your bedtime," he told her.

"But it's still today," she stated plainly, as if it were an indisputable fact. She always had a way of spinning things to her advantage, a trait she definitely didn't pick up from him.

With a burst of ten-year-old energy, she scrambled to the far end of the sofa and reached for something hidden in the shadows.

Joel had a vague idea what was coming. "Honey, please not right now. I do not have the energy for this."

Ignoring his plea, Sarah popped up and confronted him with an outstretched arm. "Here."

In her hand was a square gray box.

"What's this?" Joel reached out and took it from her.

"Your birthday," Sarah replied, again stating the obvious.

He opened the box. An overwhelming sense of appreciation swept over him and he struggled hard to contain it.

"You kept complaining about your broken watch, so I figured, you know..." She ended the sentence with a shrug.

He removed the watch and sat the box down on the coffee table. He was too exhausted to handle the feelings that threatened to reveal themselves, and so to avoid them, he focused on fastening the watch to his wrist.

"You like it?"

The truth was he loved it. But hard knocks had taught Joel to keep his emotions at arm's length, and so the protective shield went up. He tapped the watch face and - making a face - said, "Honey, this is nice, but..."

"What?" There was a trace of panic in her voice.

He held the watch up to his ear. "It's nice but I think it's stuck. It's..." He made a helpless shrug.

Instantly Sarah panicked. "No, no, no..." She grabbed his wrist as her face went pale. A second passed... a second she noted by the ticking of the hand on Joel's watch, and her color returned.

"Oh ha ha," she said, pushing his arm away. She stretched out on the sofa away from him.

"Where'd you get the money for this?"

"Drugs," she said over her shoulder. "I sell hardcore drugs."

"Oh good." He settled into the sofa and grabbed the remote. "You can start helping out with the mortgage then."

She snorted. "You wish."

* * *

After over an hour of flipping channels, decompressing from an entire day spent putting band-aids on a sinking ship, Joel switched off the television. His worries had eased, thanks to the midnight marathon episodes of real-life lumberjacks, but a few concerns still bubbled to the surface. His earlier joke to Sarah about helping out with the mortgage had a kernel of truth. He was behind on the mortgage, not to the point of imminent foreclosure, but being behind on the house payment was never a good thing.

And this business with the construction crew was troublesome. Never before had he encountered so many setbacks related to crews not showing up. A typical nail-bender like himself knows you only get paid if you do the work. Construction workers ain't salaried and they ain't protected by the union. If a guy called in sick, you could bet your ass he's laid out at home and coughing up a lung. One, two guys on a crew sick? He guessed it was possible.

But five? Six? No, there had to be something else going on. Something serious.

If you listened to the news, with its tendency to exaggerate everything, you'd think the world was coming to an end. Skyrocket admittance to hospitals, people dropping at bus stops, in check-out lines, the post-office. There was even a local story of a woman who passed out behind the wheel of her SUV and careened into a bus load of school children. Thank God the kids weren't hurt, but Jesus...

And there were other news articles lurking in between the headlines of the flu epidemic. These were much more troublesome and so Joel steered his attention away from them, but you couldn't get some of them out of your head, like "mass-hysteria" and "brutal family slaying" and the worst: "man kills wife before feasting on family dog."

Christ, he thought, watching the scrawl at the bottom of the screen before flipping the television off for good. What in the world is going on?

He looked at Sarah sleeping peacefully beside him and he fought for some comforting thoughts, thoughts to replace the troubling images swirling in his head. Tomorrow was Friday, thank God, and that meant the weekend was near. He was looking forward to Sarah's soccer game in the afternoon - she was the team's star performer. Watching her shine on the field would do a lot to alleviate the worries from his shoulders.

He struggled to his feet, scooped Sarah up in his arms and carried her off to bed.

You'll notice right away that there's a lot going on in the narration that wasn't explicitly rendered in the video. That's the nuance and subtext that you as a writer are required to give. You see, the reader can't *see* the anguish on Joel's face, so they have to experience it from your words. Your job as a writer is one of manipulating the reader, making them feel pain, joy, sadness and heartbreak. Your only tools are the words you use, but to get that feeling on the page, you must experience it yourself, in your heart and soul.

You've got to allow yourself to feel the anguish Joel feels, the absolute heartbreak of holding his daughter in his arms, before you can adequately express it on the page.

When you write, allow yourself to be sucked in by the emotions your screenplay emotes. It's the only way to truly express and impart those emotions to the reader, and trust me, they're *dying* to feel it. Whenever a book gets closed early, it's because the writer didn't manage to translate those feelings on to the page. Don't be that writer!

(If I've turned you onto THE LAST OF US, great, I know you'll enjoy the experience. If you want to follow my journey as I transform the entire game to novel, with video clips of the game to illustrate the techniques I use, then I encourage you to visit my blog: http://richardgarrison.blogspot.com)

Using ChatGPT

Need a little help to get you started?

If you're reading this in the year 2023 or later, welcome to the world of A.I. (Artificial Intelligence)! It's amazing, and a tad bit scary.

If you're so inclined, you can use A.I. to help you shorten the process of step one (converting your script to prose) by using ChatGPT, and I will show you how to do it.

You can limit how much ChatGPT will alter your prose by providing very specific instructions. Let's get to it!

First, go to chat.openai.com.

Next, start a new conversation:

[Me]
For this series of chats, I will provide you with a scene from a screenplay. I want to convert the scene into narrative prose by only changing the verb tense to past and replacing screenplay dialogue with fiction dialogue, using normal dialogue attribution tags when necessary. Understand?

[ChatGPT]

Understood! Feel free to provide the scene, and I'll convert it into narrative prose as per your instructions. Go ahead whenever you're ready!

[Me]
Here is the scene:

```
INT. DETECTIVE'S OFFICE - DAY
Jack sits before the desk of DETECTIVE
WARNER. He's young, handsome, tall. He's
dressed in a white dress shirt and tie.
Leaning up against the wall, observing, is
DETECTIVE MARTIN RAMIREZ. He's a little
older, wizened.
WARNER
So tell us again about this dream you had.
Jack fidgets uncomfortably in his chair. As
he squirms, we hear what's in his head.
JACK (V.O.)
I had decided early on, even before
entering the station, to avoid mentioning
the whole thing about the attic and the old
typewriter I'd found. For some reason,
going down that rabbit hole made me see
myself being dragged to the funny farm in a
strait-jacket, with no one to blame but
myself...
Jack clears his voice and speaks.
JACK
I woke up in the middle of the night, could
```

see what had happened pretty clearly. Like
I said, the guy from Channel Nine News was
there...
Warner interrupts.
WARNER
You wake up in the middle of the night and
you're dreaming of...
(refers to his notes)
Harold Jackson, the news anchor?
Jack looks up; the Detective's tone is
funny, almost one of ridicule.
JACK
That's right. Harold Jackson. He was there,
he went to her apartment with a purpose.
Jack glances up at the other cop, Ramirez.
The guy's face is impassive. No clue there.
JACK (CONT'D)
See, she had printed her home address on
her business cards, which I personally
thought was a bad idea, but...
RAMIREZ
(interrupting Jack)
How did you know that?
Jack tugs at his shirt collar.
JACK
What?
RAMIREZ
How did you know her business card had her
home address?
Jack stammers.
JACK
She -- she gave me one of her cards the day

we met for lunch.

RAMIREZ

A day before she was murdered.

Jack nods. An odd thought suddenly rushes
to him. We hear his internal revelation...

JACK (V.O.)

My heart was pounding in my chest. The idea
of needing an alibi suddenly popped into my
head. Why hadn't this thought occurred to
me before?? If I didn't know any better,
I'd think they were looking at me as a
suspect.

Jack swallows hard.

JACK

In the dream.

(beat)

Jackson went to her apartment and caught
her off-guard. She thought they were
supposed to meet at the gym. I guess they'd
scheduled an appointment together.

His eyes dart from Ramirez back to Warner.

JACK (CONT'D)

(encouragingly)

Maybe she had that written down somewhere,
like in a day timer or something.

Warner locks eyes with Jack. Jack feels the
pressure building, takes a deep breath.

JACK (CONT'D)

Anyway, she lets this guy in, into her
apartment, and as she finishes getting
ready, he barges into her bedroom, beats
her up and then rapes her.

Jack's gaze falls to the floor.
JACK (CONT'D)
I guess that's when he decided to take the
phone cord from beside the bed and strangle
her with it.
Jack doesn't notice (or does he?) but this
last bit of info causes both detectives to
perk up and trade glances.
WARNER
We need you to stay in town, Mr. Harrison.
JACK
Of course.
Warner stands, motions to the door. He
smiles reassuringly at Jack.
WARNER
It's just that we may have some more
questions for you. We'll be in touch.
Jack leaves the office. Outside, in the
hallway, Jack stands there alone, a little
confused and unsure. Finally, he gathers
himself and leaves.

[ChatGPT]

Here is the response:

In Detective Warner's office, Jack sat before the desk,
facing the young, handsome, and tall Detective Warner
dressed in a white dress shirt and tie. Observing from the
wall was Detective Martin Ramirez, a little older and
wizened.

"Tell us again about this dream you had," Detective Warner requested.

As Jack fidgeted uncomfortably in his chair, he couldn't help but let his thoughts wander.

"I had decided early on, even before entering the station, to avoid mentioning the whole thing about the attic and the old typewriter I'd found," Jack's inner voice narrated. "For some reason, going down that rabbit hole made me see myself being dragged to the funny farm in a strait-jacket, with no one to blame but myself..."

After clearing his throat, Jack began to speak, "I woke up in the middle of the night, and I could see what had happened pretty clearly. Like I said, the guy from Channel Nine News was there..."

Detective Warner interrupted, glancing at his notes, "You wake up in the middle of the night and dream of Harold Jackson, the news anchor?"

Jack looked up, sensing a hint of ridicule in the Detective's tone. 'That's right. Harold Jackson. He was there, he went to her apartment with a purpose."

Jack then glanced at Detective Ramirez, whose face remained impassive, revealing no clues.

"See, she had printed her home address on her business cards, which I personally thought was a bad idea, but..." Jack began.

Interrupting Jack, Detective Ramirez asked, "How did you know that? How did you know her business card had her home address?"

Jack stammered, "She -- she gave me one of her cards the day we met for lunch."

"A day before she was murdered," Ramirez pointed out. Suddenly, a thought struck Jack.

"My heart was pounding in my chest," Jack's inner voice revealed. "The idea of needing an alibi suddenly popped into my head. Why hadn't this thought occurred to me before? If I didn't know any better, I'd think they were looking at me as a suspect."

Swallowing hard, Jack continued, "In the dream... Jackson went to her apartment and caught her off-guard. She thought they were supposed to meet at the gym. I guess they'd scheduled an appointment together."

"Maybe she had that written down somewhere, like in a day timer or something," Jack added encouragingly.

Detective Warner locked eyes with Jack, applying pressure, making him take a deep breath.

"Anyway, she lets this guy in, into her apartment, and as she finishes getting ready, he barges into her bedroom, beats her up, and then rapes her," Jack revealed, his gaze falling to the floor.

This last piece of information caught the attention of both detectives, causing them to exchange glances.

"We need you to stay in town, Mr. Harrison," Detective Warner said.

"Of course," Jack replied.

Detective Warner stood, gesturing towards the door with a reassuring smile. "It's just that we may have some more questions for you. We'll be in touch."

Jack left the office and found himself standing alone in the hallway, feeling a little confused and unsure. After a moment or two, he gathered himself and left.

For subsequent scenes, you don't need to repeat the instructions. ChatGPT will remember what it needs to do. All you have to do is keep providing scenes.

I usually do so with this prompt:

[Me]
Repeat the exercise with the following scene:

And then I just cut and paste the next scene in and hit enter, and repeat scene by scene.

You might be wondering why you have to go scene by scene, as opposed to just copying and pasting your entire script.

As of summer of 2023, ChatGPT only returns around 800 words in every response. This number may increase in the future, but for now, you need to go slowly, scene-by-scene, making sure the results are what you want.

What about A.I. Originality?

As long as your prompt instructs the A.I. to **only** modify your prose to suit the bare requirements of conversion, you have nothing to worry about. You're going to edit the text anyway in the rewriting phase.

That's not to say you can't use ChatGPT with other areas of novelization.

Let's say your slugline is:

```
INT. ATTIC - NIGHT
```

Your ChatGPT prompt may look something like:

[Me]
Describe an attic with rafters and insulation

-- or –

```
INT. COURTROOM - DAY
```

[Me]
Provide a paragraph describing the courtroom of a high-profile murder case

* * *

As you play around with A.I. tools such as ChatGPT, keep in mind its limitations.

- A.I isn't perfect.

If you read the first example of the A.I.-generated scene above, you probably noticed the missing bit about the telephone cord and the villain using it to strangle the girl. ChatGPT omitted it. Why? I think it's because some descriptions of violence violate ChatGPT's content policy. You'll usually see a warning if this is the case.

- The output is limited.

Through trial and error, I determined that the response length generated from my prompts, on average, was about 700 – 800 words for each request.

That means you must provide the scenes you want to be converted into smaller chunks.

- A.I generated content is easily detectable.

Tools exist to determine if content was generated by a human or A.I. I wouldn't just copy and paste ChatGPT's response into your final draft verbatim because, frankly, that IS cheating. But you can use the A.I. as a writing partner who gives you ideas and suggestions for developing your prose.

Here is another interesting prompt you might find useful:

[Me]
I will provide a scene from a screenplay and I want you to rewrite it as though you were Charles Portis, author of True Grit. Understand?

[ChatGPT]
Understood, partner! Lay it on me, and I'll give it a rewrite with the grit of Charles Portis. Shoot!

[Me]
INT. PIT Reno stumbles upon something in

the darkness, lowers his torch and looks at
it. It's Harlan's severed arm. Greasy fat
fingers wrapped around a parchment. RENO
Well, I'll be... He steps on the wrist and
rips the map from the dead fingers that
grip it. He holds it up to the light of the
fire and examines it. RENO (CONT'D) I hope
it was worth it, Harlan. He looks at. RENO
(CONT'D) La Puerta del Infierno. Treasure
my ass. And with that he crams the map into
his pocket.

[ChatGPT]
Here's the response:

In the dim glow of the pit, Reno's stumble led him to an
eerie discovery. His torch flickers as he lowers it to examine
the morbid find before him - Harlan's severed arm, its
greasy fat fingers clutched around a tattered parchment.
Reno's reaction is stoic but revealing of a certain awe
mixed with cynicism.

"Reckon I'll be..." he mutters, grinding his boot on the
lifeless wrist and deftly prying the map from the death grip.
Holding the precious document up to the crackling fire, he
scrutinizes it, almost daring it to be worth the gruesome cost.
Reno's words carry a hint of vindication and disbelief.

"La Puerta del Infierno, huh? Treasure, my ass." He
scoffs at the idea, perhaps sensing that the journey ahead
won't be as glorious as he once dreamed. Nevertheless,
without a flinch, he folds the map and stuffs it firmly into his
pocket, determined to face whatever fate lies beyond the
gates of Hell.

Final Thoughts

Okay, so now that I've given you all the tips and tricks for novelizing your screenplay, do you want to know the **real** secret to writing a book?

Writing a book is just like running a marathon. When you first start out, you *know* there is just no way in hell you're gonna run twenty-six miles. It sounds impossible.

But, setting all those doubts aside, you lace up your running shoes and out the door you go.

At first, you may only be able to log a mile. Then two. But then something happens… you pass a milestone you've never passed before. Five miles. Six. *Seven.* Before you know it, you start to think, *Hey, maybe I can actually do this!*

Look at your novel as the start of your marathon training. Lace up those running shoes and sit yourself down at the computer. You just need to get yourself over the hump. You need to keep at it, preferably every day, and pass that last milestone. 25,000 words. 40,000 words. *50,000 words.* You will amaze yourself by what you've accomplished, and the best thing is, you'll be eager to keep going because now you've got the confidence to know that no matter what, you won't give up.

I hope I've stirred you into action and inspired you to turn that screenplay of yours into a novel. Don't let it sit on a shelf somewhere, collecting dust. It took a lot of blood, sweat and tears to write it. It was hard work. Increase its marketability by turning it into a novel. You'll enjoy doing it and at the end of the process, you'll have more than doubled your chances of getting noticed. And more importantly, you will have changed the way you look at yourself.

Remember, you can't send a **script** directly to Clint Eastwood, Mel Gibson, or Brad Pitt. I know; I've tried. Their assistants will take your script in its unopened envelope, put it in a larger envelope, and send it right back to you.

But you can have **Amazon** send your self-published book to Clint. I'm not exactly sure what he'll do with it. Maybe he'll read it while on the can one day. But he won't send it back to you, that's for sure! ☺

Good luck and keep writing.

Rick Garrison

richardgarrison.blogspot.com

Notes